NEWSEUM

OFFICIAL GUIDE

FREEDOM of PRESS

BECKON BOOKS

The Newseum's 40-foot-tall high-definition media screen in the Great Hall of News can be lowered to the floor or raised to the ceiling.

GREAT HALL OF NEWS

At the Newseum visitors are surrounded by a continuous flow of news — instant, breaking and historic news that is uncensored, diverse and free. Sometimes that news angers; sometimes it uplifts. Sometimes, the news comes at the expense of a journalist's life. In the Great Hall of News, breaking news is broadcast on one of the country's largest high-definition video screens, while the latest headlines scroll across a constantly updated news zipper. The 90-foot-high atrium also includes two icons of modern news reporting: a replica of the pioneering communications satellite ATS-1 and a Bell "JetRanger" helicopter, a type often used by local television stations.

> *"Visitors will come to Washington as tourists, but after visiting the Newseum, they will leave as better-informed citizens."*
>
> — Al Neuharth, *founder of USA Today, the Freedom Forum and the Newseum*

A replica of the ATS-1 satellite, which NASA launched in 1966, hovers high above the atrium floor.

A SATELLITE AND A SONG The Beatles debuted their song "All You Need Is Love" from a London recording studio in 1967 during the first live global television broadcast, which was made possible in part by the ATS-1 satellite.

Orientation Theaters

The journey through the Newseum begins in the Orientation Theaters, where the award-winning film "What's News?" explores the boundaries of journalism and the public's need to know. The film focuses on the role that news plays in people's lives and how news unites people around the world and across generations. Filled with powerful images of war and peace, love and hate, life and death, "What's News?" offers a glimpse of what visitors will see at the Newseum.

In 1997, a sheep named Dolly became the first cloned mammal — news that made front pages worldwide.

TIME
Will There Ever Be Another You?
A SPECIAL REPORT ON CLONING

Jackie Robinson of the Brooklyn Dodgers made news when he broke Major League Baseball's color barrier in 1947.

The film "What's News?" — playing in the Newseum's Orientation Theaters — highlights the people and events that make headlines around the world.

JOHN S. AND JAMES L. KNIGHT FOUNDATION

Knight Studio on Pennsylvania Avenue

The Knight Studio on Pennsylvania Avenue hosts programs such as ABC News's "This Week With Christiane Amanpour." This high-definition television studio also is used by other national and international media organizations. With its unobstructed view of the U.S. Capitol providing a dramatic backdrop, the studio is a popular location for network anchors and correspondents who report the news from Washington. From this studio, the Newseum can send live programs by satellite and fiber-optic cable to virtually any place on earth.

NBC News's Brian Williams interviews then-presidential candidate Barack Obama.

Christiane Amanpour of ABC News (far left) hosts her Sunday morning news show at the Newseum.

Visitors get a close-up look at the studio.

This gallery explores each of the five freedoms guaranteed by the First Amendment from their beginnings to their relevance more than 200 years later.

BONG HiTS 4 JESUS

FREEDOM OF SPEECH

MODERN ISSUES

PIVOTAL POINTS

ORIGINS

FREEDOM OF THE PRESS

MODERN ISSUES

PIVOTAL POINTS

ORIGINS

FREEDOM OF

GOT FREE

WHAT DID HE JUST SING? Some Americans wanted to ban the rock 'n' roll song "Louie Louie" in 1963 because they said the lyrics were raunchy. The FBI and the FCC investigated, but they couldn't tell if the lyrics were obscene; they couldn't understand the words.

FIRST AMENDMENT GALLERY

On Dec. 15, 1791, the first 45 words of the Bill of Rights established the First Amendment to the U.S. Constitution. For the first time in history, a constitution guaranteed its people five fundamental freedoms to protect what James Madison called "the great rights of mankind." This guarantee of rights has played a central role in expanding liberty and justice for every person in the United States. The five freedoms are inextricably linked, and they all are strengthened by a free press that remains free. "Our liberty depends on the freedom of the press," Thomas Jefferson said, "and that cannot be limited without being lost."

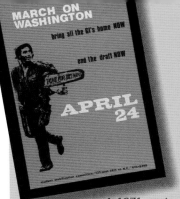

A 1971 poster for a demonstration against the Vietnam War.

Iowa siblings Mary Beth and John Tinker were suspended for wearing peace armbands to school in 1965. The Supreme Court later upheld their right to express their political opinions in school.

FREEDOM OF ASSEMBLY

The First Amendment protects the right to associate with others to advocate one's beliefs and to demonstrate peacefully. From Pennsylvania Avenue to Main Street in almost any city, demonstrations are a way for people to stand together to bring about social and political change. From civil rights to reproductive rights to religious rights, public assemblies have helped build mass movements and achieve legislative change.

FREEDOM OF SPEECH

The First Amendment guarantees the right to speak freely without government interference. Free speech comes in many forms, including art, music, books, comics, comedy, clothing, video games and the Internet. For better or worse, the First Amendment protects free expression even when it's considered offensive or distasteful. But sometimes limits have been placed on free speech.

Kentucky teen Jacqueline Duty was barred from her prom for wearing a Confederate flag–themed dress in 2004.

A student was suspended in 2002 for displaying this banner outside an Alaska high school.

Buttons worn during anti–Vietnam War protests.

FREEDOM OF THE PRESS

The First Amendment protects an independent press and prohibits the government from interfering with or censoring the media. In 1971, the U.S. government got a court order to stop *The New York Times* from publishing stories about the Pentagon Papers, a classified Vietnam War report. The Supreme Court ruled there was no justification to stop the presses, and the *Times* resumed publishing the series. Below, *Times* staff after the court's decision.

Women voted in separate ballot boxes, such as this one, before gaining the right to vote in national elections in 1920. Funds raised from the sale of thread-holders like the one above (center) were used to support suffrage efforts.

FREEDOM OF RELIGION

The First Amendment guarantees religious freedom by separating church from state and by protecting free exercise of religion. In 1938, a family of Jehovah's Witnesses was arrested after asking people on a New Haven, Conn., street if they would listen to their religious records or read their pamphlets. The Supreme Court ruled in 1940 that the state had violated their freedom of religion.

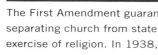

Religious records and a 1930s portable phonograph used by Jehovah's Witnesses.

FREEDOM TO PETITION

The First Amendment gives people the right to petition the government to change laws or policies. Today, petitioners often are paid lobbyists representing corporations or special interests. But not all lobbyists are paid professionals. In 1980, Candace Lightner, enraged that a drunken driver killed her daughter, founded the organization now known as Mothers Against Drunk Driving (MADD). The group's grass-roots activism resulted in the passage of many federal and state anti–drunken driving laws.

Candace Lightner's license plate.

THE PULLIAM FAMILY
Great Books Gallery

Throughout history, freedom has been the key to open and enlightened societies. It is a powerful, evolving idea. The original and rare books and documents in this gallery are some of the cornerstones of freedom — important works of political thought and action. They chart the uneven course toward democracy, tolerance and equal rights, and help illuminate the origins of freedom of the press. These books and documents were provided by The Remnant Trust, Inc. Founded by Brian Bex, the foundation strives to share the wisdom of history's greatest writings about individual liberty and human dignity.

A 16th-century English translation of the Magna Carta.

MAGNA CARTA
England, 1542

In 1215, rebellious noblemen forced King John of England to approve the Magna Carta (Great Charter). Although commoners gained little, the document guaranteed feudal rights to the aristocracy — a small but important move toward equality. Notably, one clause says that "no freeman shall be...imprisoned or exiled...except by the lawful judgment of his peers or by the law of the land." That was a crucial limitation on the king's power. This is a 16th-century English translation from Latin, the language of the original Magna Carta.

FREEDOM
"Whoever would overthrow the liberty of the nation, must begin by subduing the freedom of speech."
- Cato's Letters

In this gallery, visitors can read digital versions of the books using computer kiosks with page-turning technology.

NEWS HISTORY GALLERY

News spreads, grows and explodes. But some things never change. There will always be those who control news and those who free it, those who use it to mislead and those who use it to enlighten. The News History Gallery tells the timeless story of the need to know and the need to tell, the story of many voices struggling to be heard. It chronicles the people and machines that spread the news and the context in which they did it. The gallery also examines recurring issues that confront professional journalists, including media bias, accuracy and fairness. More than 350 historic newspapers and magazines from the Newseum collection are displayed in the gallery, along with artifacts spanning five centuries of news history.

Deadline-pressed news editors mistakenly called the 1948 presidential race for Thomas Dewey. Harry Truman, the winner, made the error famous in this memorable photograph.

The Newseum has more than 30,000 historic newspapers and magazines in its collection, featuring news from the 15th century to the present.

The News History Gallery is the largest gallery in the Newseum, with stories and artifacts covering 500 years of news.

WAR: THE BIGGEST STORY

War reporting sometimes is depicted as a romantic adventure. Occasionally it may be. More often it's dirty, depressing and dangerous — the toughest of assignments. In recent wars, journalists have been deliberately marked for death. So why are journalists drawn to war? Because few stories are more significant. Human lives and the fates of cultures and nations hang in the balance.

The Civil War marked the first time large numbers of reporters followed troops into battle. News of Abraham Lincoln's 1865 assassination, seen here in the National Police Gazette, *was transmitted by telegraph.*

War reporting came of age during World War II as hundreds of reporters, including Scripps-Howard columnist Ernie Pyle (above), covered the conflict. Pyle carried this typewriter across the battlefields of Europe and the Pacific.

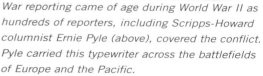

Every war brings a different set of issues, but a constant undercurrent is the struggle for information. During the run-up to the Iraq War, reporters were criticized for not asking enough tough questions.

CIVIL RIGHTS AND THE PRESS

Anyone who has had a story to tell usually has found a way to do it. Minorities used their own publications to press for voting rights and to battle discrimination. During the civil rights movement, blacks learned to use the mainstream media to expose the injustice of segregation. When Martin Luther King Jr. spoke at the 1963 March on Washington, he knew he was speaking to the entire nation through the news media.

History was made at this Greensboro, N.C., lunch counter in 1960 when a group of black college students refused to leave after being denied service in the "whites-only" section.

WOMEN AND THE NEWS

Throughout history, journalism was largely a man's world, and women were relegated mostly to lower-rung jobs with less pay. The movement of women into the workplace that began during World War II took full bloom in the 1970s. No longer would a female journalist be content to work on the "society pages" or be a "weather girl." Women moved front and center to Page One and to the anchor seat.

Elizabeth Cochrane, whose pen name was "Nellie Bly," dazzled readers with her exploits. She took this satchel on her famous around-the-world trek in 1889–90.

Morning host Katie Couric left NBC's top-rated "Today" show in 2006 to become the nation's first solo anchorwoman of a network evening newscast at CBS.

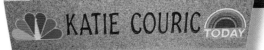

Margaret Bourke-White was the first female photographer to fly on combat missions during World War II. She used this Keystone aerial camera.

SEX! CRIME! SCANDAL!

In 1833, the penny newspaper appeared, offering sensational "scoops," grisly crime reports and harmless tall tales. The trend of embellishing stories with rumor, speculation and half-truths lives on, most notably in tabloids. But stories that have legitimate news value get overplayed or hyped in the mainstream media, too. Coverage of O.J. Simpson's arrest and trial for the murders of his ex-wife and her friend sank to new lows of sensationalism.

More than 100 million viewers saw O.J. Simpson acquitted live on television in 1995. Simpson wore this suit to court that day.

THE PRESS AS WATCHDOGS

Some journalists see themselves as watchdogs, exposing problems so society can solve them. They help protect the public from those who would do harm — from high government officials to petty criminals. *The Washington Post*'s discovery of White House involvement in the Watergate scandal helped lead to President Richard M. Nixon's resignation in 1974. But some say the press is too critical and too adversarial. Others say the news media are more like lapdogs — too timid to take on the difficult work of investigative reporting.

The Watergate scandal in the 1970s began with a break-in at the Democratic National Committee offices. Burglars had taped over the latch of this door to keep it from locking. Below, The Washington Post's Carl Bernstein (right) and Bob Woodward won a Pulitzer Prize for exposing the White House cover-up.

DIGGING UP DIRT Teddy Roosevelt coined the term "muckrakers" in 1906 to describe reform-minded reporters who uncovered social ills. The president was inspired by a character in "The Pilgrim's Progress," a man with the muck-rake who would rather look at filth on the ground than at the heavens.

Big Screen Theater

Television allows people to see and hear news as it happens. Broadcast news can expose injustice, turn the tide of public opinion and even change the course of history. The Newseum's Big Screen Theater presents historic news broadcasts, original documentaries and breaking news on a 100-foot-long video wall. By seeing multiple images simultaneously projected on the screen, visitors can relive unforgettable moments in TV history and experience new ones. Some of the most compelling and important broadcasts in history are featured in this theater, along with original productions that go behind the scenes of big news stories. When news breaks, the Big Screen Theater pulls from hundreds of news feeds from around the globe to bring visitors the latest information.

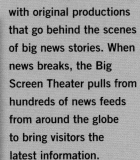

Visitors watch live newscasts in the theater.

The Big Screen Theater features original media productions, including this film on the rise of 24-hour cable news.

Daily front pages arrive electronically at the Newseum from Australia as early as 2 p.m. the day before they appear in the gallery. They continue to come in from around the world throughout the evening and the following morning.

TODAY'S FRONT PAGES

Before dawn every morning, more than 800 newspapers from around the world transmit their front pages electronically to the Newseum. Up to 80 of these front pages are enlarged and printed for display. These front pages represent each of the 50 states and the District of Columbia, as well as a sampling of international newspapers. This daily exhibit is part of the Newseum's mission to promote better public understanding of news and journalism. A front page can reveal as much about a newspaper and its community as it does about that day's news. Some days, one story dominates the front pages. But often the stories on Page One reflect the interests in the different communities the newspapers serve.

Front pages are displayed daily in front of the Newseum on Pennsylvania Avenue.

BLACK AND WHITE AND READ ALL OVER More than 1 billion people read newspapers every day. China leads the world in daily newspaper circulation with nearly 100 million readers.

"If a person goes to a country and finds their newspapers filled with nothing but good news, there are good men in jail."

— U.S. Sen. Daniel Patrick Moynihan

A view of the U.S. Capitol from the Pennsylvania Avenue Terrace.

THE HANK GREENSPUN FAMILY

Pennsylvania Avenue Terrace

Pennsylvania Avenue — "America's Main Street" — is a historic avenue of presidential parades and funeral processions, joyful celebrations and raucous demonstrations. The Newseum's Pennsylvania Avenue Terrace offers a panoramic view of one of the most famous streets in the United States. The view encompasses landmarks and monuments of American history, including the U.S. Capitol and the Washington Monument. The exhibit rail on this terrace tells the rich history of the people, events and news organizations that played a role in shaping the avenue, the city of Washington and the nation itself.

The National Hotel, where President Abraham Lincoln's assassin stayed, occupied the Newseum site on Pennsylvania Avenue from 1826 to 1942.

John F. Kennedy's 1961 inauguration was the first to be televised in color. Here, the president rides with first lady Jacqueline Kennedy in his inaugural parade.

PULITZER PRIZE PHOTOGRAPHS

With the click of a button, photographers record the defining moments of our time: the ugliness of war, the pain of poverty, the ecstasy of victory, the triumph of redemption. The Pulitzer Prize Photographs Gallery features the most comprehensive collection of Pulitzer Prize–winning photographs ever assembled. The images represent every Pulitzer Prize photography winner since 1942, when the award was first presented to Milton Brooks of *The Detroit News*. Starting in 1968, two prizes for photography — one for breaking news and one for feature photography — have been awarded every year. Inside the gallery, visitors can access more than 1,000 photographs, along with interviews with the photographers revealing how they got the pictures that were awarded journalism's most prestigious prize.

> *"If it makes you laugh, if it makes you cry, if it rips out your heart, that's a good picture."*
>
> — Eddie Adams, *Pulitzer Prize–winning photojournalist*

OLD GLORY

Iwo Jima, Japan, 1945: During one of the bloodiest battles of World War II, U.S. Marines captured Mount Suribachi. Jubilant, they raised a flag. Photographer Joe Rosenthal of the Associated Press trudged up the mountain and learned that the Marines planned to substitute a larger flag. When he noticed the men start the flag up, he used his bulky Speed Graphic camera to capture the most enduring image of the war.

FLEEING KOSOVO

Kukes, Albania, 1999: *The Washington Post*'s Carol Guzy photographed the exodus of ethnic Albanians fleeing Serb fighters in Kosovo. The makeshift camp she visited teemed with refugees coming over the border day after day. New arrivals had to wait outside until tents were set up. Barbed wire separated this refugee family. "They passed the baby back and forth," Guzy said, "just to kiss him and say hello."

The documentary film in this gallery features more than a dozen Pulitzer Prize–winning photographers telling the stories behind some of the most famous photographs of all time.

THE ANDREA DORIA

Atlantic Ocean, off Nantucket Island, Mass., 1956: The luxury liner Andrea Doria, sailing through fog-shrouded waters, was scheduled to be in New York by morning. Then the liner Stockholm collided with the ship, tearing a 40-foot hole in the Andrea Doria. Fifty-one passengers were lost. The next morning a plane circled over the wreck. Inside, Harry Trask of the *Boston Traveler* photographed the sinking ship. "In nine minutes, it was all over," he said.

Harry Trask's Graflex Speed Graphic camera.

> "I don't really take pictures. I capture and share life."
>
> — John White, *Pulitzer Prize–winning photojournalist*

HISTORIC CAMPAIGN

Chester, Pa., 2008: Damon Winter of *The New York Times* had photographed the campaign of Sen. Barack Obama for months. So he knew something special was happening when Obama showed up an hour early to a cold, rain-soaked rally. "He looked very strong, and kind of defiant," Winter said. One week later, Obama became the first African American elected president.

JOYFUL HOMECOMING

Travis Air Force Base, Calif., 1973: Families awaited the return of fathers, husbands, brothers — all American prisoners of war from North Vietnam. A giant C-141 taxied up the tarmac. The last man off was Air Force Col. Robert L. Stirm. Six years earlier he had been shot down over Hanoi. His family didn't know if they'd ever see him again. "The family had started to run toward him," Associated Press photographer Sal Veder recalled, "and that's what caught my eye."

OLYMPICS IN BARCELONA

Barcelona, Spain, 1992: Six hundred photojournalists covered the Summer Olympics, with some organizations fielding dozens of photographers. *The Dallas Morning News* sent two; they divvied up the events. Ken Geiger drew track and field. After he photographed the U.S. women winning the 100-meter relay, he noticed the Nigerians watching the scoreboard. When they learned they won the bronze, Geiger captured their moment of glory.

RETIRING NO. 3

New York, N.Y., 1948: Yankee fans were honoring baseball's Babe Ruth. The home run hero was weakened by illness, but his slow walk onto the field drove the crowd wild. *New York Herald Tribune* photographer Nat Fein took some pictures but wasn't satisfied, so he walked around to the other side. "I saw Ruth standing there with his uniform, No. 3, the number that would be retired," Fein said, "and knew that was the shot."

RUBY SHOOTS OSWALD

Dallas, Texas, 1963: *Dallas Times Herald* photographer Robert Jackson went to police headquarters to cover the transfer of suspected presidential assassin Lee Harvey Oswald to the county jail. Jackson picked his spot in the garage and pre-focused his camera. "They said, 'Here he comes,'" Jackson recalled. Then, nightclub owner Jack Ruby brushed past him and fired a gun. "I guess I fired about the same time," Jackson said.

The "I-Witness" film recreates Edward R. Murrow's live radio reports during the World War II bombing of London.

Walter and Leonore Annenberg Theater

The Walter and Leonore Annenberg Theater combines a 3-D film with special effects and motion-controlled seats to create a 4-D experience that takes visitors on a journalistic trip through time. The "I-Witness" film depicts three of history's most dramatic news events — the legendary Edward R. Murrow broadcasting from a London rooftop during World War II, Colonial journalist Isaiah Thomas witnessing the first battle of the Revolutionary War, and pioneering reporter Nellie Bly going undercover to expose abuses in a 19th-century insane asylum for women.

Actor George Clooney shares a laugh with his father, journalist Nick Clooney, during a program in the Annenberg Theater.

9/11 GALLERY

The news broke shortly before 9 a.m. on Sept. 11, 2001: A plane had crashed into the upper floors of one of the World Trade Center towers in New York City. Minutes later, a second hijacked plane hit the other tower. From New York to the Pentagon to Pennsylvania, one shocking event followed another as the news media rushed to cover the story of an unprecedented attack on the United States. As news broke in three places almost simultaneously, news organizations faced extraordinary challenges. The 9/11 Gallery tells the story of how journalists covered the events of that catastrophic day and features dramatic evidence of the attacks, including part of the broadcast antenna mast that soared atop the North Tower.

TELLING THE STORY OF 9/11

Front pages of newspapers around the globe told the story of 9/11. Searing images of the hijacked planes striking the World Trade Center and of the towers collapsing dominated most pages. More than 200 newspapers produced extra editions within hours of the attacks. Newspapers also added pages and expanded their press runs for next-day coverage. *The New York Times* sold an extra 400,000 copies on Sept. 12, 2001. The paper later won six Pulitzer Prizes for its coverage.

The Newseum's 9/11 Gallery shows the challenges journalists faced trying to report news of the terrorist attacks to the world.

> "There are three kinds of people who run toward disaster, not away: cops, firemen and reporters."
> — Rod Dreher, *newspaper columnist*

PHOTOGRAPHER LOSES HIS LIFE

Veteran photojournalist Bill Biggart was walking his dogs with his wife Wendy Doremus near their home in downtown Manhattan when he noticed an unusual cloud in the sky. Biggart ran home for his cameras and headed to the World Trade Center site. Four days later, his body was found amid the rubble of the towers. Biggart, 54, was the only journalist killed while covering the terrorist attacks.

Rescue workers recovered Bill Biggart's personal effects, including his two camera bags and three cameras, which contained nearly 300 images he shot on 9/11. Some of the film was damaged, but the digital images, including those shown at left, survived.

ATTACK ON NEW YORK

The terrorist attacks on the World Trade Center destroyed the 360-foot-tall antenna mast atop the North Tower, which served most of New York City's television stations and some radio stations. The antenna mast was constructed for the Port Authority of New York and New Jersey, which built and owned the World Trade Center. The antenna once soared 1,700 feet above the ground, making it the highest point in the city. Ten television stations lost their conventional transmission facilities when the antenna fell, but they continued to broadcast over cable lines or via satellite.

ATTACK ON THE PENTAGON

When terrorist hijackers crashed American Airlines Flight 77 into the Pentagon on Sept. 11, 2001, the Boeing 757 hit "Wedge One" — the southwest side of the building. Fifty-nine passengers and crew on the plane and 125 people inside the Pentagon were killed. When the jet struck the building, its fuel ignited. This flagpole finial, shaped like an eagle, was scorched.

PENNSYLVANIA PLANE CRASH

A fourth hijacked aircraft, the San Francisco–bound United Flight 93, had turned around and was headed toward Washington, D.C., when it crashed about 80 miles southeast of Pittsburgh. The flight, which took off that morning from Newark, N.J., carried 40 passengers and crew members. All perished in the crash, which occurred after passengers rose up against the hijackers. This piece of fuselage was recovered from the field where the plane went down.

Interactive Newsroom

News breaks, and a deadline is looming. How does a reporter prepare a complete, timely and accurate story? The Interactive Newsroom gives visitors a chance to play the role of a reporter, photographer or TV newscaster. Touch-screen stations provide the reporting tools and techniques that reveal what it takes to be a newspaper reporter or photographer. The fast-paced NewsMania game tests knowledge of current events. The Interactive Newsroom also offers visitors the opportunity to pick up a microphone, step before a camera and experience what it's like to be a TV newscaster.

Visitors have fun at the "Be a TV Reporter" experience.

BE A TV
REPORTER

In the Interactive Newsroom, visitors use touch-screen kiosks to play games that test their skills as a reporter or photographer.

Ethics Center

Each day, journalists must make tough decisions about gathering, editing and reporting the news. Should they work undercover to expose corruption? Should they try to make a photo more dramatic? At what point do they stop being reporters in order to help someone in need? These issues and more are addressed inside the Ethics Center, where examples of actual events challenge visitors to make the right call.

The game table in the Ethics Center uses motion-tracking technology and digital avatars.

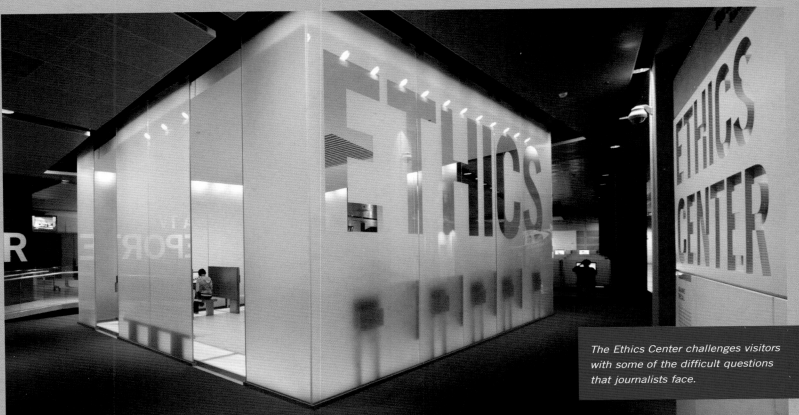

The Ethics Center challenges visitors with some of the difficult questions that journalists face.

The Internet, TV and Radio Gallery follows the development of electronic media from the birth of radio more than a century ago to today's digital news.

INTERNET, TV AND RADIO GALLERY

As technology improves, the speed of news increases. The advent of radio dramatically changed journalism, enabling people for the first time to communicate with thousands of others in a matter of moments. Television gave the news even greater impact with the addition of visual images, and satellites turned the world into an instant global village. With the Internet, the power of mass media now resides in the hands of the public. The Internet, TV and Radio Gallery traces the evolution of these three technologies and shows how they interact in delivering the news. Using electronic kiosks, visitors can access more than 70 historic radio and television broadcasts. Clips range from Franklin Delano Roosevelt's famous 1933 inaugural address to the Beatles' arrival in New York City on their first U.S. tour.

A radio announcer was testing a disc recorder in 1937 when the dirigible Hindenburg exploded. His dramatic eyewitness report was later broadcast using the new technology. Until then most news broadcasts were live.

Edward R. Murrow's pioneering live radio reporting during the Battle of Britain brought World War II into America's living rooms. This was his war correspondent's uniform.

THE AGE OF RADIO

When Japanese planes bombed Pearl Harbor in 1941, the Mutual Broadcasting System broke into its sports broadcast with a news bulletin. Within seconds, radio alerted Americans that the country was at war. Two decades earlier, the first radio newscast on a licensed commercial station came out of Pittsburgh when radio station KDKA reported the results of the presidential election on Nov. 2, 1920. By the end of the 1930s, radio had become Americans' primary source of news.

The first transistor radio, the Regency model TR-1, launched the era of consumer microelectronics in 1954.

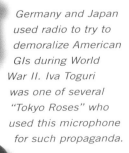

Germany and Japan used radio to try to demoralize American GIs during World War II. Iva Toguri was one of several "Tokyo Roses" who used this microphone for such propaganda.

THE RISE OF TV NEWS

With television news saturating the airwaves today, it's hard to imagine there was once only one 10-minute news program. In 1947, the DuMont Television Network started the first network TV news report. By the end of the 1950s, the number of U.S. homes with televisions was near 90 percent, and TV news was coming of age. In 1963, for the first time, more Americans got their news from television than from any other source.

THE DIGITAL REVOLUTION

Today news is transmitted by email, text messages and blogs before it ever hits the print edition of a newspaper or is broadcast on radio or television. No longer are newspapers, radio and TV the gatekeepers of news. Now that role is shared by "citizen journalists" — everyday people covering events with cellphones, digital cameras and computers.

"Never in the history of humankind has there been a medium with the impact of television. It ... literally has brought the world home in a box."
— Walter Cronkite

Television coverage of Hurricane Katrina survivors in desperate conditions shocked the world in 2005. This monitor came from a New Orleans TV news van damaged in the record flood.

Time *magazine,* 1982.

Steve Jobs revolutionized digital technology in 2010 when he introduced the iPad, a touch-screen tablet computer.

Live coverage of the Apollo 11 mission to the moon in 1969 attracted the largest TV audience to that date — more than 600 million people.

New portable TV equipment in 1963 allowed live field reports about President John F. Kennedy's assassination, letting the country watch history unfold in real time. Here, Walter Cronkite announces Kennedy's death on CBS.

Graduate student Jamal Albarghouti used this cellphone in 2007 to capture police responding to a mass shooting at Virginia Tech. His video was seen around the world.

❋ DIGITAL MUCKRAKER In 2010, the WikiLeaks website posted 76,000 classified U.S. military documents about the war in Afghanistan. It was the most substantial leak of government secrets since the Pentagon Papers during the Vietnam War.

Knight Studio

In the early days of television, studios were often crude converted spaces with low ceilings, heavy cameras that frequently broke down and lights so bright that floor temperatures could soar above 100 degrees. As technology evolved, so did broadcast studios, which today transmit a steady flow of electronic news from thousands of newsrooms worldwide. The Knight Studio is used by the Newseum to produce news and information programs, either recorded or as live telecasts. News organizations and other groups also use the studio to create high-quality broadcasts. Like the Knight Studio on Pennsylvania Avenue, this broadcast studio can be used to send live programs by satellite and fiber-optic cable to almost any place on earth.

Actor and director Robert Redford appears on NPR's "Talk of the Nation," broadcast from the Newseum.

The Knight Studio uses motorized lighting that enables a fast turnaround between studio productions.

BERLIN WALL GALLERY

In the early morning darkness of Aug. 13, 1961, the Berlin Wall appeared. Without warning, communist-controlled East Germany had strung barbed wire to seal the border around democratic West Berlin. Guards were given orders to shoot anyone trying to cross the border. More than 100 miles of fortifications and concrete barriers, including those displayed at the Newseum, later replaced the barbed wire. For 28 years, the wall stood as grim testimony to an epic confrontation between open and closed societies. But not even the wall could stop the flow of news between East Berlin and West Berlin. The Berlin Wall Gallery tells the dramatic story of how news and information helped topple tyranny to let freedom reign again.

YOU ARE LEAVING
THE AMERICAN SECTOR
ВЫ ВЫЕЗЖАЕТЕ ИЗ
АМЕРИКАНСКОГО СЕКТОРА
VOUS SORTEZ
DU SECTEUR AMERICAIN
SIE VERLASSEN DEN AMERIKANISCHEN SEKTOR
US ARMY

RISE OF THE WALL

In 1961, the only Western news agency in East Berlin was Reuters, whose bureau was run by 26-year-old Adam Kellet-Long. On Aug. 12, Kellet-Long got a mysterious phone call saying "Don't go to bed this night." After midnight, he drove toward the historic Brandenburg Gate. An East German officer stopped him, saying the border was closed. With that, Kellet-Long had the first story about the rise of the Berlin Wall.

SAVING HISTORY The director of the Checkpoint Charlie Museum in Berlin transferred the East German watchtower to the Newseum in 1994 because he feared the guard towers would be destroyed to make way for commercial development. Only a few of the towers still exist today.

Soviets said the wall was built to deter Western intrusion, but East Germans almost immediately began risking their lives to escape. Here, Artur Zimmer and 3-year-old Jörg Klein are hoisted up on a rope seat through a tunnel dug under the wall.

The Newseum's Berlin Wall Gallery explores the role of the news media during the 28-year history of the wall.

BERLIN WALL

A CITY CAGED

In the early morning darkness of Aug. 13, 1961, the Berlin Wall appeared. Without warning, communist-controlled East Germany strung barbed wire to seal the border around democratic West Berlin. Guards were ordered to shoot anyone trying to enter West Berlin. More than 100 miles of fortifications and concrete barriers, including those displayed in this gallery, later replaced the barbed wire.

The Berlin Wall was built to keep citizens in, rather than to keep an enemy out. For 28 years, it stood as grim testimony to an epic confrontation between open and closed societies.

This gallery tells the dramatic story of how news and information, which the wall could not keep out, helped topple a closed and oppressive society. ■

FALL OF THE WALL

On Nov. 9, 1989, East German authorities unexpectedly lifted travel restrictions to the West. The news spread quickly. Berliners from both sides of the city climbed over the wall and danced on top of it, sharing songs and champagne in a joyful reunion. With hammers and chisels, many pounded away at the once-fearsome barrier. After a little more than 28 years, the wall had fallen.

NBC News's Tom Brokaw reports live from the Berlin Wall after the border was opened.

A jubilant crowd at the Brandenburg Gate celebrates the opening of the border between East and West Berlin.

END OF THE SOVIET ERA

As the push for democracy in Eastern Europe accelerated, the Soviet Union's republics began breaking away, forcing President Mikhail Gorbachev to resign on Dec. 25, 1991. In his final act, Gorbachev stepped down as commander in chief and signed over control of the country's nuclear arsenal to President Boris Yeltsin of Russia. With the stroke of a pen, the Soviet era ended.

As in Berlin, citizens throughout the Soviet Union were eager to topple symbols of their oppression. Statues of Vladimir Ilyich Lenin, the architect of Soviet communism, were a popular target.

HISTORIC PEN The pen Mikhail Gorbachev used in his final act as Soviet president was lent to him by CNN President Tom Johnson after Gorbachev's pen malfunctioned. Johnson was at the event overseeing CNN's coverage.

The first name that appears on the Journalists Memorial is Elijah Parish Lovejoy, an abolitionist who was shot to death in 1837 when he tried to protect his newspaper's press from a pro-slavery mob.

Journalists Memorial

Journalists face dangers every day. Hundreds have died while covering wars and other dangerous assignments, while many others have been murdered in retaliation for their reporting. The Journalists Memorial at the Newseum honors those who died for or were killed in the pursuit of news. The two-story glass memorial bears the names of more than 2,000 reporters, photographers, broadcasters and others, including bloggers.

Each year, the memorial is rededicated with the addition of the names of journalists killed during the previous year. At the inaugural dedication, Hillary Rodham Clinton called the men and women honored by this memorial "democracy's heroes."

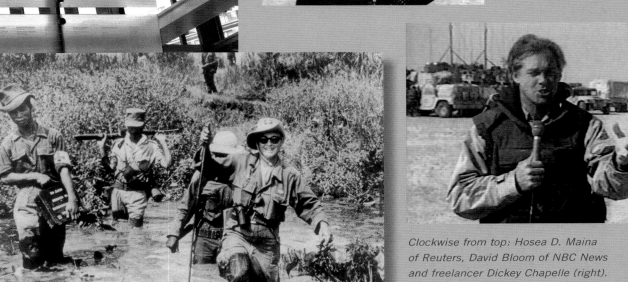

Clockwise from top: Hosea D. Maina of Reuters, David Bloom of NBC News and freelancer Dickey Chapelle (right).

A wall-size map of the world dominates the World News Gallery and provides an overview of the state of press freedom around the globe.

WORLD NEWS GALLERY

Journalists around the globe chronicle events that shape and connect our world — whether war, natural disaster or revolution. But journalists in many countries also face intimidation, censorship and dangerous conditions. They are attacked and imprisoned sometimes simply for asking a question or reporting the facts. Despite these obstacles, news still gets out, exposing the truth through the mainstream, underground and Internet press. The World News Gallery tells the stories of journalists who risked their lives to report the news. The gallery demonstrates the power of the press to spur change, and illustrates — with a vivid, wall-size map — just how precarious press freedom is in many countries around the world.

> *"News is what somebody, somewhere, wants to suppress."*
> — Lord Northcliffe, *British newspaper publisher*

FREE

PARTLY FREE

NOT FREE

WORLD PRESS FREEDOM

A majority of the world's population lives in countries without a free press. The wall map in this gallery provides a snapshot of press freedom around the world, based on data from Freedom House. The organization's annual survey shows how free the flow of news and information is in 193 countries. Ratings are determined by assessing a country's political, legal and economic climate.

A WORLD WITHOUT FREEDOM According to Freedom House, an organization that monitors freedom of the press around the world, only one in six people lives in a country where the press is considered "free."

BREAKING NEWS AROUND THE GLOBE

Technology delivers news to people at nearly the same instant all over the globe. A single news event can appear simultaneously on television, radio and the Internet. Digital technology, in particular, has transformed the way that people learn about what's happening in the world. Eyewitnesses to natural disasters now post personal videos and stories online, and activists use websites to thwart censorship and to spread word of injustice.

After their city was devastated by a tsunami in 2011, journalists at the Ishinomaki Hibi Shimbun in Japan used the only means left to report the news: pen and paper.

Egyptian authorities cracked down on massive democracy protests in 2011 by cutting Internet access.

Journalists run for cover as Libyan planes drop bombs near an oil refinery in 2011.

DATELINE: DANGER

Starting with the Crimean War in the 19th century, reporters have been on the front lines of the world's conflicts. But in return for adventure and challenge comes real danger — and, too often, death. When a country is unstable or its leaders feel offended or threatened, journalists are sometimes attacked as political enemies. They have even been targeted for assassination.

ABC News anchor Bob Woodruff was seriously injured by a roadside bomb while reporting in Iraq in 2006. He was wearing this protective body armor at the time.

These reporting tools were used by The Wall Street Journal*'s Daniel Pearl, who was kidnapped and murdered in Pakistan in 2002 while reporting on terrorism.*

SAVING LIVES While riding with an Army patrol in Baghdad in 2003, Michael Weisskopf of *Time* grabbed a grenade that was lobbed into their Humvee and tried to toss it from the vehicle. He lost his hand but saved the lives of two U.S. soldiers and photographer James Nachtwey.

This armor-reinforced truck — damaged by bullets and shrapnel — was used by Time *magazine photographer Christopher Morris in the 1990s while covering the conflict in Yugoslavia.*

CHANGING EXHIBITS GALLERY

Within the Changing Exhibits Gallery the Newseum mounts exhibits that explore compelling topics and issues in depth — taking a fresh look at important news events, news-related anniversaries and emerging media trends. The gallery's inaugural exhibit features some of the FBI's biggest cases and examines the sometimes cooperative, sometimes combative relationship between the press and the FBI during the past 100 years. Changing displays in this gallery reinforce the Newseum's commitment to illuminating how the news media work and the value of a free press.

G-MEN AND JOURNALISTS

The press was crucial to creating the FBI's carefully crafted image of using scientific methods to stamp out crime. In its early days, the FBI needed public support, and the press helped them get it. In turn, the news media used stories of sensational crime to stoke sales. But the FBI's law enforcement responsibilities and the news media's role as a government watchdog eventually put the two at odds.

One of the FBI's most famous cases was the pursuit of bank robber John Dillinger in the early 1930s. These are Dillinger's guns, bulletproof vest and personal effects, along with an FBI ledger related to the case.

The FBI exhibit examines the biggest crime stories of the bureau's first 100 years.

Federal Agents Detain Man Who
Is Believed To Be Unabom Suspect

A MAD BOMBER
AND HIS MANIFESTO

BAN THE CABIN? Unabomber Ted Kaczynski attempted to get a court to prohibit the Newseum from displaying the cabin where he hid out for 17 years and made bombs.

NEW MEDIA GALLERY

Opening soon: A new gallery at the Newseum will explore the evolving role of digital technologies in journalism and the fast-changing media landscape. The New Media Gallery will show how technology has drastically changed the collection and dissemination of news, empowering citizens while challenging traditional journalism. With a state-of-the-art design that takes advantage of the latest interactive technologies, the gallery will allow visitors to explore and experience the news as never before.

A rendering of the New Media Gallery.